Coupons For Mom
Copyright © 2020 by Lovestories Press
All rights reserved

Thank you for purchasing this coupon book
and I hope you enjoyed it.
Join Lovestories Press facebook group to
stay in the know on upcoming
releases, giveaways and a better way to
connect with us!

With love,
Lovestories Press

THIS COUPON ENTITLES THE BEARER TO

A KIDS-FREE DAY

REDEEMED BY:_______________

REDEEMED ON:_______________

OCCASION:_______________

SIGNATURE: *Lovestories Press*

THIS COUPON ENTITLES THE BEARER TO

BATHTUB AND WINE NIGHT

REDEEMED BY:_________________

REDEEMED ON:_________________

OCCASION:_________________

SIGNATURE: *Lovestories Press*

COUPON 2

Coupons for Mom

2

THIS COUPON ENTITLES THE BEARER TO

DINNER COOKED FOR ME

REDEEMED BY:________________

REDEEMED ON:________________

OCCASION:________________

SIGNATURE: *Lovestories Press*

COUPON 3

THIS COUPON ENTITLES THE BEARER TO

MOVIE NIGHT OF MY CHOICE

REDEEMED BY:_______________

REDEEMED ON:_______________

OCCASION:_______________

SIGNATURE: *Lovestories Press*

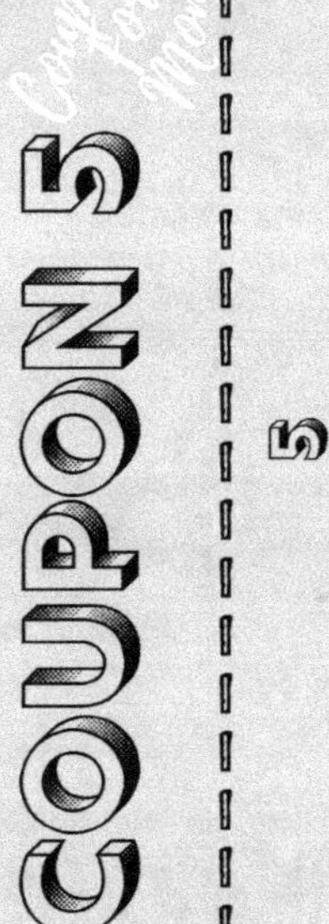

THIS COUPON ENTITLES THE BEARER TO

NO CHORES FOR MOM TODAY

REDEEMED BY:_________________

REDEEMED ON:_________________

OCCASION:_________________

SIGNATURE: *Lovestories Press*

THIS COUPON ENTITLES THE BEARER TO

START A NEW TRADITION FOR US

REDEEMED BY:________________

REDEEMED ON:________________

OCCASION:________________

SIGNATURE: *Lovestories Press*

THIS COUPON ENTITLES THE BEARER TO

A SHOPPING DAY FOR MOM

REDEEMED BY:_______________

REDEEMED ON:_______________

OCCASION:_______________

SIGNATURE: *Lovestories Press*

THIS COUPON ENTITLES THE BEARER TO

RECREATE OUR FIRST DATE

REDEEMED BY:________________

REDEEMED ON:________________

OCCASION:________________

SIGNATURE: *Lovestories Press*

THIS COUPON ENTITLES THE BEARER TO

BRUNCH WITH FRIENDS

REDEEMED BY:________________

REDEEMED ON:________________

OCCASION:________________

SIGNATURE: *Lovestories Press*

THIS COUPON ENTITLES THE BEARER TO

GAME NIGHT WITH THE WHOLE FAMILY

REDEEMED BY:_______________

REDEEMED ON:_______________

OCCASION:_______________

SIGNATURE: *Lovestories Press*

THIS COUPON ENTITLES THE BEARER TO

BUYING NEW LINGERIE

REDEEMED BY:_______________________

REDEEMED ON:_______________________

OCCASION:_______________________

SIGNATURE: *Lovestories Press*

COUPON 11

11

Coupons for Mom

THIS COUPON ENTITLES THE BEARER TO

GOING TO A SPA

REDEEMED BY:_________________

REDEEMED ON:_________________

OCCASION:_________________

SIGNATURE: *Lovestories Press*

THIS COUPON ENTITLES THE BEARER TO

AN EXOTIC NIGHT WITH MY PARTNER

REDEEMED BY:______________________

REDEEMED ON:______________________

OCCASION:______________________

SIGNATURE: *Lovestories Press*

THIS COUPON ENTITLES THE BEARER TO

EATING OUT TONIGHT

REDEEMED BY:_______________________

REDEEMED ON:_______________________

OCCASION:_______________________

SIGNATURE: *Lovestories Press*

COUPON 14

THIS COUPON ENTITLES THE BEARER TO

PLAYDATE WITH THE KIDS AND FRIENDS

REDEEMED BY:________________

REDEEMED ON:________________

OCCASION:________________

SIGNATURE: *Lovestories Press*

COUPON 15

15

THIS COUPON ENTITLES THE BEARER TO

GOING FOR A MASSAGE

REDEEMED BY:_________________

REDEEMED ON:_________________

OCCASION:_________________

SIGNATURE: *Lovestories Press*

THIS COUPON ENTITLES THE BEARER TO

A WEEKEND TRIP

REDEEMED BY:_______________________

REDEEMED ON:_______________________

OCCASION:_______________________

SIGNATURE: *Lovestories Press*

COUPON 17

Coupons For Mom

17

THIS COUPON ENTITLES THE BEARER TO

AN EVENING FULL OF SWEETS AND PASTRIES

REDEEMED BY:________________

REDEEMED ON:________________

OCCASION:________________

SIGNATURE: *Lovestories Press*

COUPON 18

THIS COUPON ENTITLES THE BEARER TO

HELP IN THE KITCHEN

REDEEMED BY:_______________

REDEEMED ON:_______________

OCCASION:_________________

SIGNATURE: *Lovestories Press*

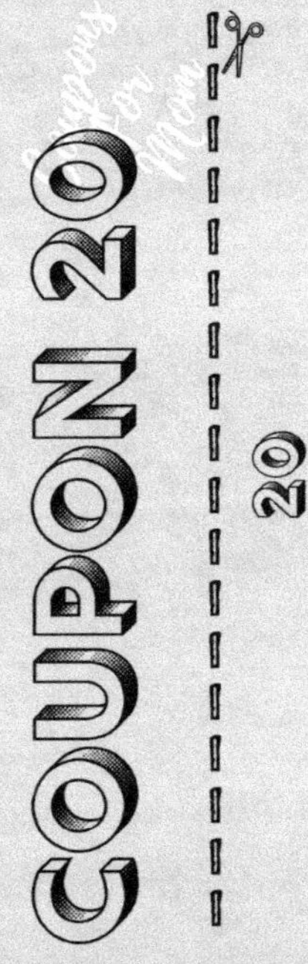

THIS COUPON ENTITLES THE BEARER TO

A NIGHT OUT

REDEEMED BY:_______________

REDEEMED ON:_______________

OCCASION:_______________

SIGNATURE: *Lovestories Press*

THIS COUPON ENTITLES THE BEARER TO

ONE BIG HUG FROM EVERYONE

REDEEMED BY: _______________________

REDEEMED ON: _______________________

OCCASION: _______________________

SIGNATURE: *Lovestories Press*

COUPON 21

THIS COUPON ENTITLES THE BEARER TO

BREAKFAST IN BED

REDEEMED BY:_______________________

REDEEMED ON:_______________________

OCCASION:_______________________

SIGNATURE: *Lovestories Press*

THIS COUPON ENTITLES THE BEARER TO

A FOOT MASSAGE

REDEEMED BY:________________

REDEEMED ON:________________

OCCASION:________________

SIGNATURE: *Lovestories Press*

THIS COUPON ENTITLES THE BEARER TO

AN AFTERNOON TO MYSELF

REDEEMED BY:＿＿＿＿＿＿＿＿＿＿

REDEEMED ON:＿＿＿＿＿＿＿＿＿＿

OCCASION:＿＿＿＿＿＿＿＿＿＿＿

SIGNATURE: *Lovestories Press*

COUPON 24

THIS COUPON ENTITLES THE BEARER TO

NETFLIX AND PIZZA

REDEEMED BY: _______________

REDEEMED ON: _______________

OCCASION: _______________

SIGNATURE: *Lovestories Press*

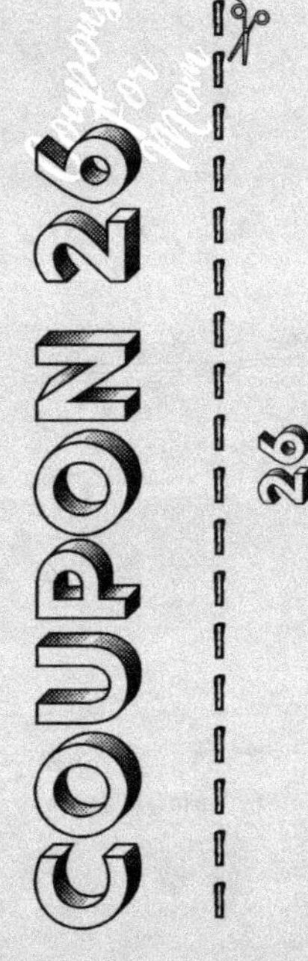

THIS COUPON ENTITLES THE BEARER TO

REDEEMED BY:______________________

REDEEMED ON:______________________

OCCASION:______________________

SIGNATURE: *Lovestories Press*

THIS COUPON ENTITLES THE BEARER TO

REDEEMED BY:_________________

REDEEMED ON:_________________

OCCASION:_________________

SIGNATURE: *Lovestories Press*

THIS COUPON ENTITLES THE BEARER TO

REDEEMED BY:________________

REDEEMED ON:________________

OCCASION:________________

SIGNATURE: *Lovestories Press*

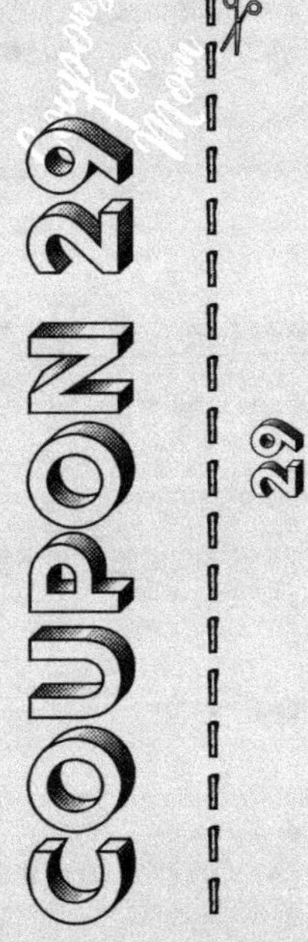

THIS COUPON ENTITLES THE BEARER TO

REDEEMED BY:_______________

REDEEMED ON:_______________

OCCASION:_________________

SIGNATURE: *Lovestories Press*

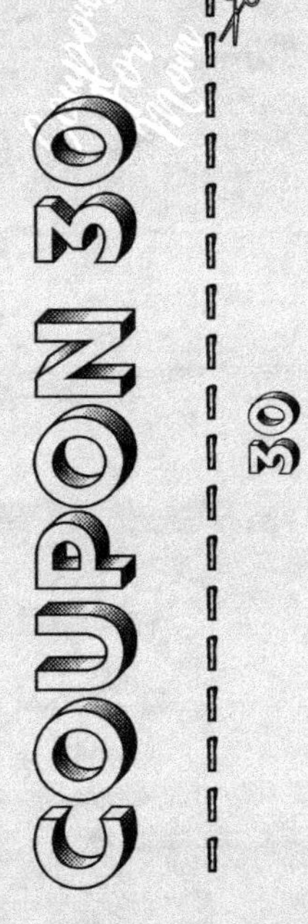

THIS COUPON ENTITLES THE BEARER TO

REDEEMED BY:________________

REDEEMED ON:________________

OCCASION:________________

SIGNATURE: *Lovestories Press*

OTHER COUPON BOOKS

Sweet and Naughty Sex Coupons

Coupons For Children